W9-ABQ-344

Amazing Civil War Nurse

CLARA BARTON

Mary Dodson Wade

AMAZING AMERICANS

Enslow Elementary

an imprint of

Enslow Publishers, Inc.

40 Industrial Road
Box 398
Berkeley Heights, NJ 07922
USA

http://www.enslow.com

Enslow Elementary, an imprint of Enslow Publishers, Inc.
Enslow Elementary® is a registered trademark of Enslow Publishers, Inc.

Library of Congress Cataloging-in-Publication Data

Wade, Mary Dodson.
    Amazing civil war nurse Clara Barton / Mary Dodson Wade.
        p. cm. — (Amazing Americans)
    Includes index.
    Summary: "An entry-level biography of Clara Barton, and the American Red Cross"—Provided
by publisher.
    ISBN-13: 978-0-7660-3281-1
    ISBN-10: 0-7660-3281-7
    1. Barton, Clara, 1821-1912—Juvenile literature. 2. American Red Cross—Biography—Juvenile
literature. 3. Nurses—United States—Biography—Juvenile literature. I. Title.
    HV569.B3W33 2009
    361.7'634092—dc22
    [B]
                                2008024889

Printed in the United States of America
052011 Lake Book Manufacturing, Inc., Melrose Park, IL
10 9 8 7 6 5 4 3 2

To Our Readers: We have done our best to make sure all Internet Addresses in this book were active and appropriate when we went to press. However, the author and the publisher have no control over and assume no liability for the material available on those Internet sites or on other Web sites they may link to. Any comments or suggestions can be sent by e-mail to comments@enslow.com or to the address on the back cover.

♻ Enslow Publishers, Inc., is committed to printing our books on recycled paper. The paper in every book contains 10% to 30% post-consumer waste (PCW). The cover board on the outside of each book contains 100% PCW. Our goal is to do our part to help young people and the environment too!

Illustration Credits: Clara Barton National Historic Site, National Park Service, pp. 4, 18; Courtesy of the Maryland State Archives, 12; FEMA photo/Andrea Booher, p. 19; The Granger Collection, New York, p. 11; Library of Congress, Prints and Photographs Division, p. 7; National Archives and Records Administration, pp. 15, 16; Ronald C. Saari, p. 8.

Cover Illustration: Clara Barton National Historic Site, National Park Service

Caption: Clara Barton, photographed around 1865 by Matthew Brady.

CONTENTS

CHAPTER 1

Growing Up

Clara Barton was born on Christmas Day in 1821. Her brother David thought she was a special present. Later, she would give a great gift to America.

◄ **Clara Barton founded the American Red Cross.**

The Bartons lived on a farm in Massachusetts. David and Clara were always together. He taught her to ride horses.

One day David was building a roof for a barn. He fell and was badly hurt. Clara was eleven. She wanted to help. She took care of David for two years until he got well.

When David was hurt, Clara helped him get better. ▶

Clara took classes to become a teacher. She started teaching when she was 17 years old. She opened the first free public school in New Jersey.

Then she went to Washington, D.C. Clara became one of the first women to work in a government office.

◄ This is the school that Clara Barton opened in Bordentown, New Jersey.

Chapter 2

The American Civil War

In 1861, the Civil War started. Soldiers from northern states fought soldiers from southern states. Some battles were near Washington, D.C.

Clara went to hospitals to take care of wounded soldiers. She collected water, food, blankets, and medicine. She brought these supplies to battlefields. Soldiers called her "The Angel of the Battlefield."

Clara helped soldiers on the battlefield and in the hospital. ▶

ROLL OF MISSING MEN.—NO. 1.

Beals, Edward A., co. C, 85th inf.
Cushman, A. P., co. H, 100th inf.
Carter, Henry A. co. A, 179th inf.
Church, Delos, co. I, 72d vol.
Carter, Henry A., co. A, 179th inf.
Canfield, Aug. W., co. D, 86th inf.
Catford, James, co. H, 13th inf.
Carson, James, 1st serg., co. D, 140th inf.
Clay, Thomas, serg., co. H, 125th inf.
Curtis, Wm. H., co. I, 146th inf.
Campbell, Jno. F., co. A, 147th inf.
Conklin, Elijah D., corp., co. —, 120th inf.
Compton, Charles W., co. —, 121st inf.
Coon, Harvey, co. A, 90th inf.
Chidester, Albert, co. H, 109th inf.
Corwin, James C., co. C, 111th inf.
Ceary, Dennis, co. A, 164th inf.
Coburn, Amasa, co. H, 106th inf.
Conklin, A. J., co. —, 120th inf.
Church, William P., co. C, 42d inf.
Clark, Oliver P., co. B, 94th inf.
Dermot, Peter, co. H, 146th inf.
Dumont, Peter L., serg., co. A, 146th inf.
Dyke, Albert, co. I, 85th inf.
Dalton, S. P., co. K, 22d inf.
Dimmick, Samuel S., co. K, 40th inf.
Durham, R. H., co. H, 123d inf.
Duff, James F., co. C, 146th inf.
Dennis, Henry G., co. D, 156th inf.
Duel, Myron A., co. E, 142d inf.
Dimmond, Frederick, co. E, 146th inf.
Duncan, David, co. K, 169th inf.
Devenhoff, I. Derr, co. B, 121st inf.
Drake, George N. L., co. G, 121st inf.
Dillon, William H., co. B, 146th inf.
Denno, William, co. A, 98th inf.
Drayton, William, co. F, 51st inf.
Doughty, Edwin F., co. A, 48th inf.
Evans, Franklin, co. D, 140th inf.
Eldred, Addison M., co. E, 52d inf.
Eddy, John C., co. E, 112th inf.
Earl, William, co. —, 60th inf.
Farley, Thomas, co. K, 148th inf.
Fleegar, Henry, co. C, 47th inf.
Fish, Hosea, co. A, 179th inf.
Finch, Thomas B., 1st serg., co. C, 108th inf.
Forges, William, co. I, 40th inf.
Fralick, William, serg., co. I, 97th inf.
Fisher, H. C., co. —, 69th inf.
Fuller, Nelson T., co. E, 51st inf.
Forger, William, jr., co. —, 40th inf.
Farrar, Charles, co. A, 12th inf.
Fairfax, Charles, co. A, 111th inf.
Garner, Charles M., co. I, 97th inf.
Garrett, S. J., co. D, 146th inf.
Graves, S. G., co. H, 20th inf.
Graves, William T., co. H, 20th inf.
Graves, Robert T., co. F, 146th inf.
Goffe, John W., co. G, 146th inf.
Goodman, B. F., serg., co. B, 57th inf.
Gardner, Charles, co. I, 97th inf.
Hillis, Joseph, co. D, 167th inf.
Hart, William, co. B, 94th inf.
Horton, Nathan S., co. —, 49th inf.
Hecker, George, co. —, 40th inf.
Holley, Theodore W., co. —, 76th inf.
Hayes, John, co. K, 140th inf.
Hudson, William T., co. K, 85th inf.
Hudson, John A., co. A, 148th inf.
Hyer, Albert, co. A, 157th inf.
Haner, Stephen, serg., co. C, 109th inf.
Holloway, Jos. H., co. D, 146th inf.
Hadsall, Isaiah, co. B, 146th inf.
Hunter, William, co. E, 162d inf.
Holmes, Eugene S., co. K, 117th inf.
Hodges, Charles, co. G, 121st inf.
Hughes, George, ord. serg., co. C, 89th inf.
Henry, James, serg., co. I, 76th inf.
Hecker, George, co. —, 40th inf.
Hermans, F. C., co. A, 20th inf.
Hayward, S. S., co. C, 67th inf.
Haner, David, co. G, 134th inf.
Hyne, William, co. D, 140th inf.
Hudson, John, co. A, 148th inf.
Hugh, E. G., co. C, 140th inf.
Howard, John, co. H, 111th inf.
Howard, Leverett, 118th inf.
Howell, William H., corp., co. E, 124th inf.
Irish, E. W., 1st serg., co. C, 85th inf.
Johnson, James T., co. A, 104th inf.
Jones, David W., co. C, 115th inf.
Johnson, E. W., co. —, 50th eng.
Johnson, Thomas A., co. K, 179th inf.
Jones, Ezra C., co. E, 147th inf.
Johnston, William, co. —, 140th inf.
Jones, Daniel W., co. C, 115th inf.
Jones, George, co. —, 100th inf.
Jerome, James, co. F, 111th inf.
Kelley, Lutheran, co. —, 149th inf.
Kelley, Thomas, co. —, 59th inf.
Keating, Michael, co. A, 146th inf.
Keeler, Elijah K., co. C, 70th inf.
Knight, Arthur F., co. F, 117th inf.
Kessler, John A., co. B, 149th inf.
Kidder, William, co. H, 8th inf.
Keating, Thomas, co. L, 83d inf.
Lach, William, co. E, 100th inf.
Lynch, Joseph, co. A, 117th inf.
Leroy, Lineberg, co. —, 128th inf.
Longee, John L., co. H, 139th inf.
Lansdell, Joseph, co. A, 95th inf.
Latham, Sylvester, co. I, 96th inf.
Lutton, Thomas, co. —, 95th inf.
Loll, Gaylor, co. C, 152d inf.
Lall, G. H., co. H, 152d inf.
La Boiteaux, Wm., co. K, 148th inf.
Miller, Samuel W., co. K, 131st inf.
McNeill, D. C., serg., co. E, 159th inf.
McPherson, Alex., co. G, 121st inf.
Madan, Wm. H., co. G, 162d inf.
Morey, Wm. D., co. F, 152d inf.
Mailer, James R., serg., co. B, 134th inf.
Mills, Jay J., co. E, 85th inf.
Marsh, Chas. R., co. E, 142d inf.
Maurice, Pigotte, co. K, 170th inf.
McCormick, John, serg., co. A, 162d vol.
Merrill, M. C., co. G, 118th vol.
McElroy, Wm., co. B, 121st vol.
Main, Wm. Oscar, co. A, 85th vol.
Merkle, Jos., co. A, 1st vol. Excel. brig.
Morgan, D. V. B., co. E, 93d vol.
McQuilkins, Thos., co. I, 1st vol.
May, Horace, co. D, 118th vol.
McMichael, James, co. H, 66th vol.
Murphy, Peter, co. K, 74th vol.
Martin, E. W., co. B, 16th vol.
McOmber, Otis, co. B, 76th vol.
Marsh, Edwin T., co. I, 140th vol.
Norwicke, A. J., corp., co. B, 156th vol.
Northrop, J. B., co. —, 111th vol.
Nelson, John H., co. D, 14th vol.
Ogden, Stephen T., co. G, 111th vol.
Olmstead, J. W., co. —, 69th vol.
Prosser, E. W., co. A, 64th vol.
Peters, George, co. A, 111th vol.
Parsons, Warren B., co. E, 64th vol.
Rodney, Pasho, co. I, 51st vol.
Persons, Henry, co. C, 40th vol.
Poor, Elijah, co. —, 92d vol.
Page, Ozias D., co. F, 146th vol.

Porter, Geo. A., co. K, 14th vol., Brooklyn.
Potter, Henry, co. E, 48th vol.
Quackenbush, George, co. —, 94th vol.
Reiley, John J., co. C, 69th vol.
Remington, Henry, co. C, 122d vol.
Reeve, George, co. C, 152d vol.
Ripley, Fras. A., serg., co. C, 152d vol.
Rickett, Wm., co. F, 97th vol.
Rockafeller, W. E., co. D, 85th vol.
Russell, Geo. R., co. D, 117th vol.
Radley, John, co. C, 152d vol.
Rockwell, Eldridge, co. I, 42d vol.
Stone, Alvat B., co. A, 94th vol.
Seymour, Fred., co. D, 156th vol.
Scheidler, George, co. F, 97th vol.
Snyder, K. L., co. D, 85th vol.
Smith, George, co. K, 111th vol.
Smith, Andrew, co. F, 160th vol.
Sherwood, Jones, co. G, 70th vol.
Sergent, Stanly, co. C, 152d vol.
Sherman, A. E., co. A, 117th vol.
Smith, William S., co. —, 85th vol.
Seward, A. R., co. D, 76th vol.
Scholl, Henry, co. —, 146th vol.
Smalley, George D., co. H, 140th vol.
Stockwell, Lewis, co. H, 97th vol.
Seiler, Jno. T., co. F, 140th vol.
Sleeger, Geo. B., co. A, 94th vol.
Schott, Henry, co. —, 146th vol.
Sampson, Thomas S., co. G, 92d inf.
Snook, James S., co. A, 51st inf.
Stevens, Wm. Thomas, co. I, 20th inf.
Smith, James, co. K, 104th inf.
Stannard, W. W., co. D, 118th inf.
Shearman, A. R., co. F, 179th inf.
Salyer, Simeon, co. C, 126th inf.
Swanson, James, co. E, 146th inf.
Smith, George, co. K, 111th inf.
Stevens, F. L., serg. 12d, cons'd with 120th inf.
Shuyler, Henry S., co. I, 86th inf.
Tidd, Samuel V., co. K, 124th inf.
Taylor, Stephen, co. G, 97th inf.
Tilford, Braton P., co. F, 149th inf.
Taylor, Thomas J., co. B, 93d inf.
Thomas, James L., co. A, 104th inf.
Trousdell, Wm. J., co. I, 140th inf.
Taylor, Levi, co. H, 69th inf.
Taylor, Adney, co. H, 69th inf.
Tuttle, James C., co. D, 16th inf.
Taylor, Charles, co. F, 115th inf.
Taylor, Lorenzo D., co. D, 141st inf.
Terwilliger, Nelson, co. C, 120th inf.
Taylor, S. B., co. K, 147th inf.
Upham, Jared Jewel, 85th inf.
Vorhis, Jacob, co. F, 104th inf.
Vannasdall, Wesley D., co. A, 115th inf.
Van Blarcom, Isaac, co. D, 95th inf.
Van Schuyver, George, co. G, 108th inf.
Van Arman, Charles E., co. H, 69th inf.
Vantine, G. G., co. F, 106th inf.
Vale, Adrian, serg., co. D, 176th inf.
Williams, John, drummer, 226th inf.
Wellen, Augustus P., co. B, 100th inf.
Wisner, Wm. Owen, co. I, 49th inf.
Williams, John H., co. C, 58th inf.
Webster, Elwood, co. K, 76th inf.
Westcott, Henry C., co. F, 118th inf.
Wiley, James, co. B, 59th inf.
West, Wm. W., co. D, 157th inf.
Woodward, Oran B., co. I, 111th inf.
Wolf, John, co. E, 111th inf.
White, George W., co. F, 104th inf.
Wilson, Robert, co. A, 117th inf.
Weller, John J., co. E, 63d inf.
Wiser, M. L., co. F, 90th inf.
Waldron, Nelson, co. K, 176th inf.
Wallace, Thomas, serg., co. G, 164th inf.
Whitten, Joseph G., co. I, 120th inf.
Wolfe, Cristian A., co. D, 132d inf.
Warren, Nathan T., co. I, 105th inf.
Williams, A. B., serg., co. D, 111th inf.
White, H. G., co. A, 94th inf.
Williams, Lyman W., co. F, 121st inf.
Wilson, James, co. K, 132d inf.
Webb, Lewis M., co. F, 147th inf.
White, Lois, co. D, 156th inf.
Yeta, Charles, co. A, 121st inf.

Alexander, Ephraim, jr., co. —, 15th cav.
Atwell, Theodore, serg., co. M, 6th cav.
Bentley, Washington, co. —, 25th cav.
Bishop, Chester, corp., co. B, 10th cav.
Borst, Edwin, co. B, 5th cav.
Breese, Niles, co. H, 3d cav.
Barr, John, serg., co. F, 10th cav.
Bowman, Byron J., co. E, 10th cav.
Briggs, Benjamin T., co. F, 12th cav.
Bacon, Lyman, co. E, 8th cav.
Burke, John, co. D, 2d cav.
Boyce, Ambrose A., co. I, 3d cav.
Bixby, Daniel C., co. —, 5th cav.
Bross, N. D., co. H, 3d cav.
Bayliss, Edward, co. C, 24th cav.
Bootey, John C., co. C, 9th cav.
Baker, Lamont M., serg., co. G, 24th cav.
Bronson, Marcus D., co. B, 6th cav.
Barr, John, serg., co. F, 10th cav.
Borden, Holland, corp., co. —, 3d cav.
Baker, Josiah, co. M, 15th cav.
Boorman, John H, co. D, 1st cav.
Bingham, Charles Elmer, co. D, 5th cav.
Coleman, James H., serg., co. C, 3d cav.
Caly, Herschell, co. L, 21st cav.
Cremer, Martin, co. F, 15th cav.
Chase, Samuel, co. L, 2d cav.
Carpenter, John, co. C, 22d cav.
Dougherty, William, co. B, 5th cav.
Dewes, Thomas, serg., co. K, 22d cav.
Davis, Henry T., co. G, 5th cav.
Evens, Luke, co. G, 22d cav.
Estes, E. M., co. —, 3d cav.
Elmendorf, Alex. F., co. —, 2d Harris light cav.
Farnham, Charles F., co. G, 5th cav.
Farnham, Frederic, co. F, 6th cav.
Failing, Milton M., co. C, 8th cav.
Gleason, Harrison D., co. M, 22d cav.
Garrigan, Edward C., co. F, 2d cav.
Gorton, Cornelius, co. B, 5th cav.
Gifford, Edwin M., co. A, 3d cav.
Getman, David, co. I, 10th cav.
Hazen, John M., co. G, 5th cav.
Hubbard, John, co. —, 8th cav.
Hughes, John H., serg., co. H, 24th cav.
Harvey, Barton J., co. D, 6th cav.
Huson, George B., co. —, 22d cav.
Hecks, Fred., co. —, 5th cav.
Hill, Andrew J., co. M, 15th cav.
Hopson, Sidney P., 6th cav.
Jackson, John W., co. F, 5th cav.
Kerk, Edw., co. —, 18th cav.
Kenney, Michael, co. F, 12th cav.
Keys, Davenport, co. B, 5th cav.
Lamson, Henry, co. M, 15th cav.
LaGrange, Caspar, co. G, 10th cav.
Latham, Eldridge P., serg., co. H, 6th cav.
Lyon, Charles, co. K, 21st cav.
Munroe, George, co. F, 5th cav.
Miner, William B., co. —, 4th cav.
Mix, Albert J., co. A, 12th cav.
Morgan, Edwin L., co. F, 12th cav.
Main, Milo A., co. G, 10th cav.

Moohler, John, co. E, 2d cav.
Monroe, George, co. K, 4th cav.
Miller, Rockwell L., co. C, 5th cav.
Miner, Henry, serg., co. K, 5th cav.
Mahan, Benjamin F., co. K, 5th cav.
McMinn, Clarence L., co. E, 3d cav.
Norton, Ashbel, co. M, 15th cav.
Niemann, William H., serg., co. F, 5th cav.
Patterson, Orim, co. E, 24th cav.
Perine, Joseph L., co. D, 25th cav.
Pratt, George B., co. D, 10th cav.
Pread, Simeon G., co. D, 13th cav.
Raymond, William O., co. L, 8th cav.
Ray, George C., co. D, 2d cav.
Rustin, James W., co. D, 8th cav.
Riggs, Hiram M., co. D, 13th cav.
Rossett, Edward, co. —, 5th cav.
Smith, Robert H., corporal, co. E, 3d cav.
Smith, William F., co. J, 5th cav.
Smith, Volney L., co. L, 4th cav.
Smith, Charles, serg., co. E, 9th cav.
Southworth, Robert, serg., co. E, 22d cav.
Smith, James, co. M, 24th cav.
Smith, James A., co. H, 22d cav.
Salisbury, Edwin, co. D, 16th cav.
Segar, Edwin, co. F, 8th cav.
Stearns, Alvin, co. D, 6th cav.
Smith, Leroy S., lieut., co. G, 14th cav.
Terry, Scudder H., co. K, 13th cav.
Taylor, Alexander, co. —, 5th cav.
Trussler, J. C., serg., co. F, 9th cav.
Winnett, Jos. A., co. —, 8th cav.
Woodhull, David F., co. E, 8th cav.
White, Martin, co. I, 18th cav.
Whipple, Marion D., co. D, 22d cav.
Watson, Thomas, co. —, 22d cav.
Warner, Adna M., co. A, 8th cav.
Wynkoop, Gay, co. H, 10th cav.
Youngs, G. C., co. H, 23d cav.
Heath, Jarius P., co. D, 2d vet. cav.
Johnson, George W., co. H, 1st vet. cav.
Jones, John B., co. D, 1st vet. cav.
Roe, Henry, co. F, 1st vet. cav.
Bowen, Wm. B., co. H, 1st N. Y. drag.
Buckley, Samuel F., co. —, 2d mounted rifles.
Jones, William, co. F, 2d mounted rifles.
Ames, James R., co. I, 14th heavy art.
Allen, David H., co. F, 4th heavy art.
Baily, Robert, co. —, 8th heavy art.
Bayne, Henry C., co. A, 8th heavy art.
Bayne, George W., co. A, 8th heavy art.
Brown, Oscar, co. A, 9th heavy art.
Boss, George T., co. D, 9th heavy art.
Blodget, A. T., co. H, 4th heavy art.
Barbey, John, co. L, 2d heavy art.
Bedell, George D., 12th battery.
Brown, Edwin F., corp., co. A, 8th heavy art.
Burr, Frank H., co. —, 2d heavy art.
Brown, James Ira, co. H, 5th heavy art.
Bishop, Cassius M. C., co. M, 7th heavy art.
Blodgett, Frederick, co. D, 5th heavy art.
Clark, Ira A., co. —, 8th heavy art.
Carloss, Edwin M., serg., co. L, 14th heavy art.
Calvert, Walter L., co. I, 8th heavy art.
Cole, Edgar, co. D, 14th heavy art.
Cross, Asa, co. M, 4th heavy art.
Cook, Frank, co. F, 4th heavy art.
Church, Zenas E., co. C, 4th heavy art.
Crosby, Horace M., co. B, 5th heavy art.
Downs, Valentine J., co. A, 2d heavy art.
Dewitt, John E., co. —, 4th heavy art.
Dunham, Russell, co. C, 8th heavy art.
Drew, Hiram, co. F, 4th heavy art.
Devendorf, Rudolph, co. L, 2d heavy art.
Dygert, Warner N., co. D, 2d heavy art.
Ellis, William, co. E, 2d heavy art.
Fay, John W., co. A, 8th heavy art.
Foley, Thomas, co. E, 2d heavy art.
Fish, Lester N., co. H, 7th heavy art.
Foster, Charles S., co. I, 7th heavy art.
Faulkner, Richard, co. E, 8th heavy art.
Garfield, George, co. H, 7th heavy art.
Gerald, Frederick, co. E, 8th heavy art.
Gillett, William, co. I, 8th heavy art.
Houghtaling, Jacob H., co. E, 7th heavy art.
Holmes, Wm. S., co. K, 8th heavy art.
Hertsberg, Otto, co. E, 8th heavy art.
Jaffers, Benjamin, co. D, 9th heavy art.
Jones, David, co. —, 9th heavy art.
Johnson, George W., co. —, 8th heavy art.
Kenyon, Franklin A., co. —, 8th heavy art.
Kahle, Christian, co. D, 8th heavy art.
Lyon, James, 5th independent battery.
Leonard, Chas. H., co. A, 7th heavy art.
Longstaff, John Wm., co. B, 8th heavy art.
Loomis, John, co. M, 14th heavy art.
Lester, Wm. C., co. G, 5th heavy art.
Ladue, Ambrose, co. E, 9th heavy art.
Laflare, John, co. A, 14th heavy art.
Lake, Romantus, co. B, 4th heavy art.
Lock, John B., serg., co. L, 7th heavy art.
McCollum, Melvin C., co. F, 8th heavy art.
Marsh, Chas. co. H, 4th heavy art.
Marcellus, Lewis, co. A, 9th heavy art.
Murray, James E., co. D, 8th heavy art.
Mosier, Edward, co. E, 9th heavy art.
McConnell, Evi, co. E, 9th heavy art.
Moshure, Abijah, co. G, 7th heavy art.
Martindale, Wm. J., co. D, 5th heavy art.
Owen, Chas. G., co. M, 14th heavy art.
Pearson, James, co. E, 8th heavy art.
Parker, Orren F., co. A, 8th heavy art.
Phelps, G. S., co. A, 14th heavy art.
Pope, Joseph, co. G, 2d heavy art.
Rumsey, George W., co. F, 5th heavy art.
Richards, Jas. M., co. G, 5th heavy art.
Rogers, Amos, co. I, 7th heavy art.
Rose, Adelbert, co. H, 5th heavy art.
Reily, Henry, 15th heavy art.
Rose, Elsler, co. H, 4th heavy art.
Rawson, Porter D., 24th battery.
Stiles, Geo. W., co. I, 7th heavy art.
Stapleton, Richard, co. C, 7th heavy art.
Simmons, Almon B., co. H, 8th heavy art.
Spaulding, Mortimer, co. B, 14th heavy art.
Sykes, N. B., co. H, 4th heavy art.
Smith, John D., co. G, 4th heavy art.
Scheidler, George, co. F, 17th New York.
Satterlee, John, co. E, 4th heavy art.
Thornton, Judson M., co. A, 14th heavy art.
Toll, Reinhard, co. C, 14th heavy art.
Travis, Harrison, co. G, 4th heavy art.
Thomas, John E., co. H, 5th heavy art.
Tucker, James, co. C, 9th heavy art.
Way, David, co. D, 9th heavy art.
Waring, William E., co. A, 4th heavy art.
Wilson, Simon, 4th heavy art.
Whritemour, Marcus, co. M, 15th heavy art.
Woolsey, John, 24th bat.
Wright, John W., co. L, 2d heavy art.
Watson, James, 8th heavy art.
Weeks, William, co. D, 8th heavy art.
Weldon, John, co. E, 7th heavy art.

STATE OF NEW JERSEY.

Arnold, Edwin B., co. —, 33d inf.
Bailey, William B., co. C, 15th inf.
Bloodgood, Augustus, co. —, 11th inf.
Dickerson, William C., co. D, 15th inf.
Dougherty, John W., co. H, 7th inf.
Dunn, George W., co. F, 1st inf.
Egbert, James co. B, 15th inf.
Finnon, James, co. I, 11th inf.
Griggs, Thomas, co. —, 33d inf.
Howard, Thomas H., co. H, 10th inf.
Hyde, Wilson, co. B, 38th inf.
Lipscy, Jacob M., co. I, 10th inf.
Lovell, W. F. co. D, 1st inf.
Minion, Jacob P., co. B, 15th inf.
Muchmore, Elias D., co. C, 14th inf.
Miller, Henry, co. B, 38th inf.
Reid, JoT., co. D, 14th inf.
Shipley, Andrew J., co. C, 8th inf.
Thorne, Charles D., co. E, 10th inf.
Turner, Peter, co. K, 4th inf.
Wells, Charles J., co. C, 10th inf.
Woods, W. S., co. D, 1st inf.
Wright, W. H., co. K, 1st inf.
Wilson, Harrison, co. E, 10th inf.

Carrie, W. J., co. —, 2d cav.
Eberd, Ernest, co. —, 3d cav., hussars.
Hulmes, Edward, co. M, 2d cav.
Melick, George A., co. E, 2d cav.
McPeck, Henry P., co. B, 1st cav.
Peterson, Henry, co. H, 3d cav.
Skill, Charles W., co. M, 3d cav.
Williams, Charles J., co. L, 1st cav.

PENNSYLVANIA.

Aikman, William, co. F, 116th vol.
Anthony, J. C., co. A, 56th vol.
Axtell, J. G., co. A, 145th vol.
Andrew, David W., co. D, 26th vol.
Byers, Samuel, co. D, 62d vol.
Button, Charles, co. B, 149th vol.
Black, Samuel N., co. F, 106th vol.
Bigelow, Charles A. W., co. F, 53d vol.
Bechtell, Isaac, co. A, 184th vol.
Buckley, William, co. B, 90th vol.
Bower, George W., co. K, 103d vol.
Briggs, Theron T., co. B, 145th vol.
Burdick, Charles W., co. C, 145th vol.
Boryer, S. P., co. I, 111th vol.
Bond, ——, co. I, 183d vol.
Bice, James, co. —, 149th vol.
Barnes, Walter, co. G, 119th vol.
Burton, Joseph N., co. A, 61st vol.
Barnes, H. J., co. A, 57th vol.
Brock, Jacob, co. F, 103d vol.
Bennett, Byron, co. —, 141st vol.
Burns, John, co. A, 83d vol.
Bender, Flavius G., co. C, 77th vol.
Brubaker, Benjamin, co. D, 79th vol.
Coppersmith, Jno. P., co. I, 145th vol.
Criswell, Sherman M., co. B, 103d vol.
Copp, William, co. I, 143d vol.
Campbell, Amos, co. C, 11th vol.
Clark, John, co. G, 103d vol.
Conley, M. L., co. E, 138th vol.
Cowan, Espy, co. G, 191st vol.
Casserly, Thomas, co. G, 191st vol.
Campbell, Knox G., co. G, 191st vol.
Corbet, James, co. H, 99th vol.
Chamberlain, James, co. H, 107th vol.
Clemens, Wm. D., co. B, 88th vol.
Conley, Wm., co. B, 95th vol.
Colebaugh, Wm., co. K, 99th vol.
Carr, Wm. E., co. E, 149th vol.
Diehl, Espy, co. D, 55th vol.
Dimpsey, John H., co. A, 63d vol.
Dix, Edwin, co. C, 83d vol.
Dick, James, co. —, 79th vol.
Dunlap, S. A., co. I, 103d vol.
Dermit, Eben, co. F, 116th vol.
Deffbaugh, Wm. H., co. E, 138th vol.
Deffbaugh, Jno. W., co. A, 184th vol.
Delaney, Matthew, co. B, 51st vol.
Davidson, Alex., co. G, 191st vol.
Dale, Solomon, co. D, 148th vol.
Drumm, Michael H., co. C, 85th vol.
Draved, George C., co. C, 81st vol.
Ehrenfeld, J. M., co. D, 184th vol.
Eberhart, James W., co. G, 191st vol.
Ekes, Ezekiel, co. E, 103d vol.
Ellinger, John, co. I, 107th vol.
Eckendorff, George R., co. A, 157th vol.
Elben, William, co. I, 69th vol.
Etters, David, co. D, 148th vol.
Etters, Francis W., co. A, 13th vol.
Etters, Henry, co. A, 13th vol.
Freed, George W., co. H, 148th vol.
Finley, Joseph, co. F, 48th vol.
Fay, Stephen, co. —, 106th vol.
Foster, Frank, co. H, 143d vol.
Fisher, John, co. I, 85th vol.
Gass, John T., co. D, 22d vol.
Gilbert, Henry, co. F, 53d vol.
Greer, W. Henry D., co. K, 141st vol.
Gee, W. H. L., co. H, 45th vol.
Guyst, J. W., co. I, 57th vol.
Green, Joseph F., co. H, 105th vol.
Grim, Henry, co. K, 48th vol.
Gibson, David, co. A, 55th vol.
Gordon, Robert, co. G, 69th vol.
Houston, Will., co. D, 10th vol.
Hunt, John T., co. K, 55th vol.
Hyatt, Thomas J., co. K, 118th vol.
Hyatt, James W., co. H, 118th vol.
Hershey, Abraham L., co. G, 2d vol.
Hall, John, co. B, 100th vol.
Hill, Wilson S., co. D, 141st vol.
Hill, Charles F., co. C, 72d vol.
Hern, Robert, co. I, 111th vol.
Housel, William P., co. —, 190th vol.
Hess, Levi, co. —, 118th vol.
Heisley, F. A., co. G, 191st vol.
Haley, James B., co. —, 100th vol.
Host, Jacob, co. G, 83d vol.
Hoover, John, co. —, 155th vol.
Hendershot, David, co. E, 143d vol.
Howye, Matthew, co. E, 141st vol.
Hamilton, John E., co. H, 188th vol.
Hagan, George, co. —, 199th vol.
Hudson, Thomas E., co. K, 48th vol.
Hall, John, co. B, 100th vol.
Hawk, Michael, co. F, 103d vol.
Johnson, James E., co. I, 45th vol.
Jones, James, co. K, 9th vol.
Johnson, Harris, co. I, 45th vol.
Klinger, Ephraim, co. H, 148th vol.
Kecker, David, co. A, 184th vol.
Kelly, Henry, co. F, 138th vol.
Keyser, Jacob, co. B, 148th vol.
Kerskosky, Julius, co. H, 50th vol.
Knox, James, co. A, 184th vol.
Kratzer, H., co. F, 76th vol.
Kinsley, Nathan P., co. H, 145th vol.
Kell, Jordan, co. F, 118th vol.
Karns, Jacob J., co. K, 149th vol.
King, John L., co. E, 118th vol.
Kers, John Oliver, co. F, 100th vol.
Kelley, George W., co. I, 101st vol.
Kephart, Samuel, co. C, 77th vol.
King, Daniel, co. B, 84th vol.
Kneep, Peter, co. —, 149th vol.
Layton, Samuel, co. A, 184th vol.
Learn, Adam, co. E, 11th vol.
Lake, Fred., co. F, 106th vol.
Luther, Burton K., co. —, 52d vol.
Letteer, Alfred W., co. —, 77th vol.
Livingston, George W., co. H, 190th vol.
Lee, George W., co. I, 67th vol.
Munsell, Harvey M., co. C, 99th vol.
Metcalf, Wm. H., co. —, 87th vol.
McGuire, Richard P., co. A, 55th vol.
Morse, Levi, co. F, 141st vol.
Meinhard, Ferdinand, co. H, 50th vol.
McCoy, A. J., co. I, 103d vol.
McCoy, Shannon, co. F, 138th vol.
Masters, ——, co. —, 143d vol.
McDowell, John S., co. F, 77th vol.
Miller, Orlando O., co. B, 145th vol.
McKee, Charles W., co. H, 191st vol.
Margus, Edwin, co. C, 63d vol.
Miller, Herman K., co. H, 148th vol.
McKinnon, John Y., co. H, 53d vol.
Marks, William H., co. D, 118th vol.
Morton, George H., co. I, 118th vol.
Moody, Oscar A., co. G, 150th vol.
Morris, William, co. G, 77th vol.
Matthews, F. A., co. C, 148th vol.
McCarthy, David, co. D, 68th vol.
Musser, John, co. D, 77th vol.
Moore, Joseph H., co. E, 72d vol.
Malone, Albert M., co. E, 106th vol.
Mellon, William, co. A, 106th vol.
Meldrum, John C., co. C, 184th vol.
McConnell, Philip J., co. I, 55th vol.
Martin, Alvin A., co. D, 53d vol.
Moorhead, Howard S., co. H, 101st vol.
McNess, John H., co. E, 100th vol.
McGill, George, co. K, 45th vol.
Neal, George B., co. G, 188th vol.
Noble, James H., co. D, 73d vol.
Ober, David S., co. A, 184th vol.
Obonnor, Hugh J., co. A, 49th vol.
Oliver, George C., co. D, 111th vol.
Oler, James, co. D, 101st vol.
Orbin, Thomas, co. B, 85th vol.
Potter, James O., co. G, 53d vol.
Purdy, William, co. H, 149th vol.
Potter, Benj. F., co. I, 148th vol.
Pierce, Byron, co. K, 141st vol.
Parent, Philip, co. —, 45th vol.
Purcell, Patrick, co. K, 101st vol.
Phipps, Joseph A., co. E, 57th vol.
Parker, William H., co. D, 102d vol.
Quance, Charles H., co. H, 145th vol.
Rauch, Simon, co. E, 148th vol.
Rhinehardt, Samuel, co. I, 107th vol.
Russell, Ernest F., co. I, 141st vol.
Rhodes, William H., co. I, 145th vol.
Riddell, Royal W., co. C, 145th vol.
Raynolds, Charles R., co. H, 145th vol.
Rowland, Masters, co. F, 111th vol.
Sandt, Edward, co. A, 47th vol.
Smith, Wilbur, co. I, 82d vol.
Smith, William, co. F, 84th vol.
Sardam, Francis, co. D, 53d vol.
Scoutan, Lewis, co. F, 53d vol.
Smith, Job, co. A, 140th vol.
Starks, Charles T., co. —, 149th vol.
Stotler, Thomas, co. —, 101st vol.
Shirk, John H., co. —, 79th vol.
Scavercoll, James, co. K, 141st vol.
Shaffer, John, co. —, 57th vol.
Steel, Joseph, co. B, 191st vol.
Sayre, James, co. I, 10th vol.
Steere, Charles, co. E, 95th vol.
Sharp, Martin L., co. F, 100th vol.
Sheriff, Charles F., co. K, 100th vol.
Stevens, George H., co. G, 77th vol.
Sorber, Andrew, co. F, 53d vol.
Trout, Jacob W., co. K, 138th vol.
Turner, James W., co. A, 211th vol.
Teeter, Christian S., co. A, 184th vol.
Tripp, George W., co. E, 143d vol.
Tillotson, Perry H., co. K, 57th vol.
Thompson, Joseph S., co. H, 183d vol.
Thompson, Cowden, co. I, 10th vol.
Truman, W. W., co. G, 191st vol.
Vancuren, Edward, co. C, 145th vol.
Vail, Gilbert B., co. G, 77th vol.
Vail, Merritt J., co. B, 143d vol.
Ward, Samuel, co. H, 135th vol.
Walker, Houston, co. E, 100th vol.
Wolford, Wm., co. B, 149th vol.
Wickerham, W. H. H., co. D, 22d vol.
Wilber, Louis W., co. D, 106th vol.
Warner, Edwin A., co. D, 85th vol.
Woodcock, Thomas, co. E, 183d vol.
Welch, Robert, co. I, 101st vol.
Wright, Edmund S., co. A, 184th vol.
Williams, John E., co. B, 62d vol.
Wilson, James, co. K, 83d vol.
Wheaton, Ambrose H., co. G, 53d vol.
Wilkinson, John, co. I, 45th vol.
Weeks, William, co. F, 75th vol.
Wolford, William H., co. B, 149th vol.
Whitson, Henry, co. H, 53d vol.
Whitney, Orange P., co. H, 187th vol.
Young, John, co. —, 149th vol.
Young, John, co. C, 45th vol.
Young, Philip S., co. H, 101st vol.

Aikelo, John J., co. H, 5th cav.
Austin, Edward, co. F, 20th cav.
Black, James A., co. D, 14th cav.
Bryan, William C., co. D, 5th cav.
Beardsley, Luther, co. L, 12th cav.
Baker, Willard, co. L, 12th cav.
Bevens, Robert, co. I, 20th cav.
Brady, Michael, co. M, 5th cav.
Brosius, Amos P., co. K, 14th cav.
Cormer, Abner P., co. B, 4th cav.
Campbell, Thomas F, co. B, 4th cav.
Coleman, J. L., co. K, 18th cav.
Davis, James, co. I, 5th cav.
Deming, Charles W., co. D, 16th cav.
Dyer, Joshua E., co. D, 5th cav.
Evans, Samuel F., co. F, 7th cav.
Ellis, Enos, co. I, 11th cav.
Foot, Charles, co. G, 20th cav.
Fuller, Henry, co. M, 13th cav.
Gillmore, Robert A., co. —, 12th cav.
George, Thomas, co. B, 18th cav.
Gass, John F., co. C, Ringgold battalion.
Gates, Jacob S., co. D, 13th cav.
Geary, G. S., co. D, 4th cav.
Havens, John, co. L, 19th cav.
Hottenstein, George W., co. I, 18th cav.
Hennigh, Nathan L. H., co. A, 14th cav.
Hart, Isaac, co. B, 17th cav.
Havlin, Matthew, co. D, 4th cav.
Ivory, Thomas, co. G, 12th cav.
Jones, Henry P., co. B, 2d cav.
Kelley, George W., co. K, 18th cav.
Lane, Amos P., co. B, 6th cav.
Levan, John, co. G, 8th cav.
Lobb, Nathan, co. L, 6th cav.
Miller, Lewis, serg., co. L, 6th cav.
Morgret, William, co. K, 18th cav.
McCray, Charles E., co. B, 12th cav.
Mugot, John, co. K, 18th cav.
Miller, Hamlin B., co. I, 14th cav.
McFadden, Lewis, co. L, 4th cav.
Malaby, Aaron H., co. B, 7th cav.
Meckley, Eli, co. E, 17th cav.
Miller, William, co. L, 6th cav.
Myers, Joseph M., co. D, 13th cav.
McCoy, Isaac A., co. A, 9th cav.
Mastezatt, Charles A., co. D, 14th cav.
Meredith, Alfred A., co. A, 22d cav.
McCoy, Alexander, co. A, 9th cav.
Meredith, Alfred A.,
Norris, John G., co.
Neifergold, Henry,
Nagel, George W.,
Norris, Simon, co.
Odenheimer, John
Oliver, Adam E., co.
Penepacker, Benj. F.
Ramsey, Milton G.,
Rudd, William, co.
Robbins, James, co.
Ruper, Emanuel, co.
Rees, David T., co.
Sellers, John T., co.
Smith, Samuel A., co
Smith, James L., co.
Swearer, George N.,
Schmidt, Charles L.,
Shields, William, co.
Schlearback, Conrad,
Snowden, John W.,
Scott, Andrew J., co.
Smith, Dennis, co. A,
Sanderson, Wm. E.,
Sargent, C. B., co. F,
Siebert, John, co. B,
Watkins, Andrew, co.
Woodburn, James S.,
White, George, co. C,
Wallace, Frank, co. F
Walker, James W., co
White, Joseph, co. A,
Wright, Jacob, co. B,
Young, George H., co
Bail, Joseph L., co. F,
Bird, George, co. F, 2
Beaner, Simon J., co.
Crawford, Sylvester,
Claybaugh, Geo. W.,
Hartwick, John, co. C
Hansinger, Aaron, co.
Irvin, Charles, co. G,
Miller, Eden, co. K, 2
Ormsby, C. M., co. G,
Ordning, George, co.
Rogers, Jeremiah B.,
Simpson, John D., co.
Towson, Jeremiah B.,
Wood, James M., co.
Wood, George H., co.
Bragg, Lucian G., co.
Belcher, Geo. W., co.
Davison, Garrett, co.
Huston, Wm. S., co.
Hinkel, Jonas, co. C,
Jayne, S. W., co. C,
Lathrop, Halsey, co. C
Laino, John, co. D, 10
Laughten, Robert E.,
McCurdy, John G., co
McCahon, James, co.
McPark, Robert, co. I
Margut, Mathia, co. D
McCloy, John, co. F,
Otto, John, co. F, 7th
Seaton, M. A., co. G,
Stansbury, Y. S., co.
Smith, G. W., co. H,
Welty, Jacob W., co.
Woodburn, Jos. D.,
Williamson, Alvin, co.

Buchanan, Julius,
Gillespie, James,
McClintock, James P.
McDowell, B. C., co.
Mulleson, John H., co
Roberts, Frederick T.
Snyder, Jacob, co. E,
Sickles, C. T., co. K,

STATE OF

Maxworthy, George
Rhine, Joseph, co. G.
Thorn, Henry T., co.

STATE OF

Duke, Cornelius, co.
German, Stephen, co.
Goriff, J. C., co. —,
Hitchins, Joseph H.,
King, Albert, co. H,
King, William J., co.
Martin, Loos, co. A,
Mervine, John, co. H
Poffinbarger, Charles
Rohrer, W. H., co. —
Seeger, Charles, co.
Wehn, George C., co

DISTRICT

Boissonnault, M. F.,
Cushing, James B.,
Giddings, Henry, co.
Jones, John, co. L, B
Maffit, E. C., co. I, 1
Overlock, R. L., co.
Smith, William E., co
Shafer, Frederick, co.
Tibbetts, John, co. I,

STATE

Allen, A. B., co. C, 1
Allen, Albert B., co.
Alward, Alfred L., co
Amour, W. Henry,
Brown, James E., co.
Brown, Henry H., co.
Beard, Osro R., co. —
Blocher, Henry D, co.
Batley, George, co. C
Cowels, George, 10th
Crane, John B., co. D
Connally, John, co. H
Cahill, Wm. F., co. A
Cram, John B, co. D,
Cary, Asa, co. E, 21st
Cayle, James P., co.
Clay, Oliver D., co. G
Coit, Eureka, co. C 1
Davis, Clinton W., co
Dodge, David B, co.
Duffy, James, co. H,
Ells, Henry M, co. G,
Ewing, David, co. D,
Gurnsey, Chas. W.,
Hillyer, John H., co.
Harsh, Christian, co.
Henderson, David, co.
King, John P., co. C,
Kerr, Andrew, co. I,
Joselyn, Alfred A., co
Johnson, Samuel G.,
Lee, H. D., 32d reg.
McPurdy, James, co.
McCollum, Jas. Madis
McNaury, F. G., co.
Maher, Patrick, co. E,
Moorehead, Josiah, co
McPurdy, James, co.
Moore, Chas., co. I,
Presban, James A., co.

After the war, many soldiers did not come home. People knew Clara had been at the battles. Families wrote to her. Had she seen their sons or husbands?

Clara made a list with the names of 22,000 dead soldiers. She put the names in newspapers or wrote letters to families. People were able to learn what happened to their missing loved ones.

◄ **Clara sent lists of missing soldiers all over the United States.**

13

Clara gave speeches about her work. She did not like to speak in front of large groups. But she did it anyway. Then she got sick and lost her voice.

Clara gave speeches to raise money. She used the money to find out what had happened to the missing soldiers.

CHAPTER 3

Founding the American Red Cross

Clara traveled to Europe to get well. She learned about a group called the International Red Cross that helped people during wars.

In 1881, Clara founded the American Red Cross. This new group would help people during wars or when natural disasters ruined homes.

◄ The American Red Cross helped soldiers during World War I. Here, a worker serves lunch to soldiers.

Clara Barton died when she was 90. Her lasting gift to millions of Americans was the American Red Cross.

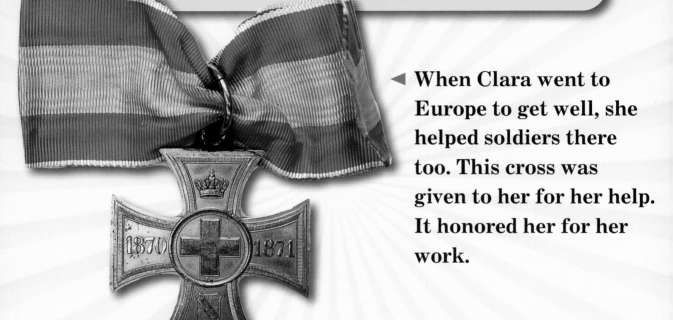

◄ When Clara went to Europe to get well, she helped soldiers there too. This cross was given to her for her help. It honored her for her work.

The American Red Cross still helps people today. This volunteer is helping after Hurricane Katrina in 2005. ►

SOMETHING TO THINK ABOUT

Clara Barton said, "*While our soldiers can stand and fight, I can stand and feed and nurse them.*"

Do you think she was wise to go to the battlefield? Was she brave? What is the bravest thing you have ever done?

Clara Barton said that she did not like to be told about old ways of doing things. She wanted to try new ways to make things better.

How did she change things for the better?

TIMELINE

1821—December 25, born in North Oxford, Massachusetts.

1852—Established first free public school in New Jersey.

1854—Began work in U.S. patent office.

1862—Allowed to go to battlefield to nurse wounded soldiers.

1865—Helped families find out what happened to missing soldiers.

1869—Went to Europe, learned about the International Red Cross there.

1881—Established the American Red Cross.

1912—April 12, died in Glen Echo, Maryland.

WORDS TO KNOW

battles—When soldiers fight.

Civil War—The war between the Northern and Southern states of the United States from 1861 to 1865.

disaster—Something bad that happens, like a storm that kills people and ruins homes.

medicine—Drugs to help sick people get well.

soldiers—People who are in the army to fight in wars.

wounded—To be hurt.

★ LEARN MORE

BOOKS

Koestler-Grack, Rachel A. *The Story of Clara Barton*. Philadelphia: Chelsea Clubhouse, 2004.

Raum, Elizabeth. *Clara Barton*. Chicago: Heinemann Library, 2004.

Schaefer, Lola M. *Clara Barton*. Mankato, MN: Pebble Books, 2007.

INTERNET ADDRESSES

American Red Cross
http://www.redcross.org

Clara Barton Birthplace Museum
http://www.clarabartonbirthplace.org/

PLACES TO VISIT

Clara Barton NHS
5801 Oxford Road
Glen Echo, Maryland 20812

INDEX